D1316190

Daring to Be
Ourselves

Daring to Be
Ourselves

Influential Women Share Insights
on Courage, Happiness,
and Finding Your Own Voice

From Interviews by
Marianne Schnall

Blue Mountain Press™
Boulder, Colorado

Dedication

To my daughters, Jazmin and Lotus.

Some of the selections in this book first appeared in the *Huffington Post*, the Women's Media Center, *Glamour*, *Entertainment Weekly's* EW.com, and *O, the Oprah Magazine*.

Library of Congress Control Number: 2010025029
ISBN: 978-1-59842-532-1

▉ and Blue Mountain Press are registered in U.S. Patent and Trademark Office.
Certain trademarks are used under license.

Printed in China.
First Printing: 2010

✪ This book is printed on recycled paper.

This book is printed on paper that has been specially produced to be acid free (neutral pH) and contains no groundwood or unbleached pulp. It conforms with the requirements of the American National Standards Institute, Inc., so as to ensure that this book will last and be enjoyed by future generations.

Library of Congress Cataloging-in-Publication Data

Schnall, Marianne.
  Daring to be ourselves : influential women share insights on courage, happiness, and finding your own voice / from interviews by Marianne Schnall.
      p. cm.
  Includes bibliographical references.
  ISBN 978-1-59842-532-1 (trade pbk. : alk. paper) 1. Women—Interviews. 2. Feminism. 3. Courage. 4. Happiness. 5. Self-confidence. I. Title.
  HQ1161.S37 2010
  305.42092'2—dc22

2010025029

Blue Mountain Arts, Inc.
P.O. Box 4549, Boulder, Colorado 80306

Contents

Introduction

In my career as a writer and reporter, I have had the pleasure of interviewing some of the most influential and courageous women of our time. I thank them all for allowing me the opportunity to interview them and for sharing with me their insights and life lessons, which I know they graciously offered in the hopes of helping or inspiring others. Their words of wisdom have certainly helped guide and inform me, and my hope is that they'll do the same for you.

As my catalog of interviews grew over the years, it became apparent that within each interview there were jewels of wisdom—quotes that stood out because they were so insightful or eloquent and contained timeless truths and powerful messages. I felt that a larger and more focused vehicle was calling to be born. What was calling out was this book, which has been a joyous labor of love for me. There is such collective power in having the quotes all appear together in one place.

The title of this book was inspired by a quote from Cambodian activist and author Loung Ung, who told me, "Courage is when you dare to be yourself." I kept hearing that same theme over and over from the women I interviewed: the importance of simply "being who we are." While just being ourselves shouldn't have to be a "daring" act, it can certainly feel that way for women in today's society. From girlhood on, we are often confronted by pressures to conform to ideas of who we should be rather than honoring and accepting who we actually are. As women, we must learn to trust our instincts and inner wisdom, not only for our own personal well-being, happiness, and wholeness, but also in order to express our true power and individual special gifts in the world.

While on the surface it may appear that the women in this book are so different, it becomes obvious when they start delving into their inner landscapes, experiences, and hopes and dreams as women how much we all have in common. We can feel our connection to them, our interdependence, our "oneness." Even though many of these women are very well known and accomplished, that superficial hierarchy disappears and we become a family of women, sisters, mothers, and daughters. I hope that the experience of reading *Daring to Be Ourselves* will feel like an intimate conversation with dear friends whose words provide you with thought-provoking, invaluable insights.

In addition to my hope of nourishing your soul with this book, my wish is to help awaken readers to a sense of their own beauty and inner power—in order to lead fulfilling, meaningful lives and contribute to positive change in the world.

— Marianne Schnall

Together, Women Are Strong

I advocate that every woman be a part of a circle that meets at least once a month or, if you can't do that, once every two months or every four months. But you have to have a circle, a group of people—smart, wise, can-do women—who are in the world doing their work, and you need to meet with them as often as you can so that they can see what you're doing and who you are, and you can see the same. And you can talk to each other about the world and about your lives in a circle of trust and safety. It's crucial. It is crucial for our psychological health and our spiritual growth. It's essential.

—Alice Walker

If we're by ourselves we come to feel crazy and alone. We need to make alternate families of small groups of women who support each other, talk to each other regularly, can speak their truths and their experiences and find they're not alone in them, that other women have them, too.... It makes such a huge difference.

—Gloria Steinem

When women get together as a group, it's immensely powerful.

—Annie Lennox

9

I really enjoy being together with a group of like-minded women and kindred spirits. It's especially important, I think, at this time because there are so many things going on out there in our world. We get so caught up in all these different issues—whether it's the economy, the war, the oil crisis, or the election—that sometimes we forget about the challenges women face every day. It's important to come together and to reconnect on that level.

— Loung Ung

It's so important that [women] look each other in the eye and go, "What's happening is not okay, and we are not alone in trying to shift it. We are not alone in our pain, and we are not alone in our transforming our pain into power." To see it on a global level, truly, it reminds us how much work there still is to do, and it reminds us we're all doing it. And we can support each other in doing it.

— Kerry Washington

When women hear each other's stories, told from the heart, it gives us great inspiration to keep on going.

— Elizabeth Lesser

I think that it is very important for women to help each other. It is hard to be the only woman in the room. Having a support system is very important. When I was in office, I had a group of women foreign ministers that were my friends throughout the world…. So I think there has to be the sense that once you have climbed the ladder of success, that you don't push it away from the building—you are only strengthened if there are more women.

— Madeleine Albright

Sisters: talk to each other, be connected and informed, form women's circles, share your stories, work together, and take risks. Together we are invincible. There is nothing to be afraid of.

— Isabel Allende

What Message Would You Most Want to Instill in Young Girls?

The message I would most want to instill is: you are more powerful than you know; you are beautiful just as you are.

— Melissa Etheridge

That each of them is already a unique and valuable person when she's born; every human being is.

— Gloria Steinem

Courage. Also, I encourage courtesy — to accept nothing less than courtesy and to give nothing less than courtesy. If we accept being talked to any kind of a way, then we are telling ourselves we are not quite worth the best. And if we have the effrontery to talk to anybody with less than courtesy, we tell ourselves and the world we are not very intelligent.

— Maya Angelou

*W*e need to help them really internalize the message that good enough is good enough. We don't need to be perfect. We're not supposed to be perfect; we're supposed to be complete. And you can't be complete if you're trying to be perfect.

— Jane Fonda

*T*hat they're beautiful. That they are so important and worthy, and that they need to safeguard themselves from the messages that are out there. That our society, for the most part, when it deals with or talks about women's bodies is *wrong*. That you don't have to be a size zero. You don't have to look like a *Gossip Girl* to be beautiful. That you don't have to be like one of these bone-skinny actresses. You *can* be, if that's how you naturally are, but you don't have to strive for that. That they're all beautiful, and that any woman has the right to be beautiful and that you can claim this for yourself.

— Margaret Cho

I just want to awaken [young girls] to know how much power they have. I know it sounds cliché, but I want them to know just the power of vision—because if you can see it, you can get there. I think a lot of times a lot of people are lost: they just don't believe they can do it. And if you just make one step toward it, you can. Just envision that person you would want to be.

— Charreah Jackson

When I worked with students in high schools, I advised them to learn to argue well and not be afraid of confrontations, not be afraid to disagree. If some guy or teacher is not treating you well, you have a right to speak up! You don't have to lock it away. You don't have to pretend it doesn't hurt. But you have to speak up in a way that is powerful. Write it down, practice, rehearse your lines if you need to, but please say something! Because if you don't, twenty years later you will still be thinking about it: "Well, I should have said this to him." I think we all have those experiences, and hopefully we have less of them now.

— Loung Ung

$\mathcal{D}$on't doubt…. Don't doubt what you know.

— Kerry Washington

I think it would be: trust your own outrage. I think my parents did a really incredible job of making me know that my emotional reactions to the world or to ideas or to other people were valid and valuable…. There was respect for the idea that when your gut tells you something is wrong, you trust that—and that it's not just for you, it's for other people who might not be able to be in touch with their guts in the same way or speak as loudly or as clearly as you might be able to. Part of your responsibility as just a person who cares about people is to trust your own outrage and speak out about it.

— Courtney E. Martin

Courage Is When
We Dare to Be Ourselves

Courage is a state of mind, of fearlessness, of being fearless. And we can be this on a daily basis. It takes courage to step out of your skin, to step out of your role, to step out of the society's roles for you. Especially as women, and in my case as a minority woman raised in a society where you are rarely seen and seldom heard, it took courage to step out of that role and to know that when you take that step, you will be frowned upon by your community and disappoint your family and friends. Courage is when you dare to be yourself, in whatever ways you want to be—to not be afraid, to just do it.

— Loung Ung

Women have always been courageous. They are the bravest of the brave! They are always fearless when protecting their children, and in the last century, they have been fearless in the fight for their rights.

— Isabel Allende

If it's not as easy as we thought it was for women to speak our truth, to even know our truth, then the missing ingredient is some sort of inner courage. To first of all believe in the validity of who we are and then to speak from it… it takes inner courage. As a leader in a large organization, I've often been the only woman working with powerful men, especially when I was younger. It really honed in me a courage to go out on a limb and demand to be heard in the only way that I really knew how to speak: from my female voice, that "different voice." Because if we try to speak in a voice that isn't ours, we lose our power.

Sometimes to speak as a woman is to cry and to speak from our emotional, intuitive knowing, as opposed to graphs and charts and vertical lines. And that's scary—that's scary to do—and the fallout from it can be brutal, and then it's scary to go on. I'm interested in helping women become courageous in being exactly who they are, because the only way to change anything is to do it from your genuine self.

— Elizabeth Lesser

Speaking Our Truth

Give voice to what you know to be true, and do not be afraid of being disliked or exiled. I think that's the hard work of standing up for what you see.

— Eve Ensler

Huge pressures are brought to bear on women to dismiss a truthful voice as "stupid"… or to hear it as crazy or to see it as bad or selfish or wrong. So we know that [truthful] voice; it's just we've covered it with a label, which—as we start to kind of reach for it or it starts to come up—we've been inducted into a culture that would have us dismiss that voice….

So what happens is the human voice gets shut down—earlier in boys, later in girls—and that human voice to me, right now, is absolutely crucial if humans and the planet and life on Earth are going to survive! The good news is that voice is in each of us, and we all know it. It's accessible. The bad news is there are both psychologically and politically huge forces against listening to that voice.

— Carol Gilligan

There is a point, and it's usually around puberty and when you are becoming a woman—that transition time—where women do lose their voice…. If we could save them the time lost between that time and the time when they start to regain it, can you imagine the power we would unleash? It's why most of my work now is in mentoring. Because that's a way of doing it one-on-one, one-to-twenty, however I can do it. I spend a lot of time on college campuses, a lot of time mentoring young women in all sectors of business, because I don't want them to spend as much time to get their voice as I did.

—Pat Mitchell

It took me quite a long time to develop a voice, and now that I have it, I am not going to be silent.

—Madeleine Albright

We have to break through silence and speak our truth.

—Jane Fonda

What Is the Source of Your Energy?

Love. I have a lot of love… and I feel very keenly that things could be so much better for so many more people and for so many more creatures and for the earth—I just know that. I just know it can be better and that people have it in them to rise to that. I know they do. Sometimes it's just a matter of touching that place that can be opened to the reality that we can do so much more than we think we can. My deepest desire is for people and the world to be happy. I will always believe this is possible and seek to learn how I can contribute. I have felt deeply blessed to have the vehicle of words, of voice.

— Alice Walker

Is it that I have grandchildren and I'm so upset about what we've done to their future? Is it that I love the wilderness and I'm so upset to see it disappearing? Is it because I've lived long enough to understand the horrors of things like nuclear war and chemical spills? I don't know. But there is something almost every day that makes me quite passionate, so I'm trying to create change.

— Jane Goodall

I enjoy life. I think it's fun. I try to create every moment that I can to just have fun and be with the people that I love and do things that I'm passionate about. And that's my choice. That's my decision to do that. Everybody can do it; anyone can do it.

— Cameron Diaz

My driving force is that I want to make a difference.... I feel that I have been so blessed that it is incumbent upon me to really get in there and help to make a difference for other people.

— Madeleine Albright

The source of all my energy is other people—mostly women, but some men, too. I'm very lucky because I *can* work full time at what I love and care about, so I am constantly able to talk to people who care about similar things. It's much more difficult for women who are in families that oppose them, who are in offices that ridicule them. I have a community wherever I go.

— Gloria Steinem

I think of things historically a lot of the time. I am always thinking in the future, but I'm also very aware of my grandmother, and ten generations before, that they had so little. So I am always like, "Wow. Look at how far we've come in just a little bit of time." I think that always pushes me to realize that this really isn't just my life. You really are standing on some shoulders, and you have some weight to pull—like all those things that you just enjoy, someone had to fight for that. So it just motivates me and keeps me questioning myself and my actions. And you never feel like you've done enough or that you've done anything—though you have—but it pushes you.

— Charreah Jackson

I think that I have a profound desire to undo what was done to me and to make sure it isn't done to anyone else. And I think I have a profound desire to really see if it's possible for us to evolve out of a violent paradigm, out of a violent mentality, and to actually know what the world would be like if we weren't living in that. I'm very curious about it. So I think the idea that we are murdering and dropping bombs on people... the idea that there are women across this planet who have no rights and cannot live their lives even a quarter of the way they should be living, the idea that there are people starving and living in dust, the idea that people have no voice and no life—and that this is the only life we get—gets me up and gets me going every day.

— Eve Ensler

Advice on Creating Change in the World

First of all, change is like a house: you can't build it from the top down, only from the bottom up. Whatever small change we make will be like a pebble in a pond. It will reverberate outward, and also it will be fun.... We're meant to be active and contribute to the world. What's the alternative? Just sitting there and wondering, "Oh, if I had just done this, maybe...." I've learned only one thing: no matter how hard it is to do it, it's harder *not* to do it. Then you're stuck with wondering, "What if I had said...? What if I had done...?"

— Gloria Steinem

Everybody has the power to make changes... and every change makes a difference.

— Cameron Diaz

As much as you can do helps. You don't have to be perfect, you don't have to be an expert, you don't have to have hours and hours of free time or tons and tons of money. You don't have to go to workshops to know about it. All you have to do is have faith in your passion, and it really makes your life a lot better. You feel like you're making a difference.

— Kathy Najimy

I never said, "Ooh, I want to be an activist." I just found that the more I spoke the truth, the more activist I became. I am constantly amazed at how courageous and radical speaking the truth is. The most activist thing you can do is just speak the truth and search for the truth and just follow that trail, and it will come to you. Believe me, the universe will hand it to you.

— Melissa Etheridge

There's so much to do that you will be paralyzed if you sit around thinking, "What's the best thing I can do? Or the most effective? Or who's the neediest?" These are questions that actually don't serve us. What serves us is to just pay attention to where we feel really called… I think it's less about figuring out what's the best thing to do or who's the most needy, and it's really about who are you, what are the resources you bring, and how can you match that with what the world needs?

— Courtney E. Martin

There's always something to do—always.

— Alice Walker

I think when people say to me, "Jane, I really want to help. What can I do?" people could just spend time, a bit of time each day, thinking about the consequences of their choices. Like what do you eat? Well, that may seem simple—I ate this or that today—but where did it come from, how many miles did it travel, did it harm the environment, how much pesticide was used, was it produced using child slave labor? If it was intensive farming, how did that affect the animals? How did it affect the environment, and how did it affect your health? The same with what you wear, how you travel, how you connect with people. If people would just start thinking about the consequences of all these small actions.

— Jane Goodall

You could sit there and say, "Oh, the problem's too big, I'll never be able to change it." That's a cop-out. It's a responsibility to your brothers and sisters in the world. That should be your number-one concern. You are responsible for what this world is and how it is and all it is. And if you don't want to help fix it, you're part of the problem.

— Betty Williams

With a global population of 6.8 billion people, that's a lot of potential for good to happen. If we all just do a little something, it'll go a long way. We need to realize that we are powerful beings. We live in a world where ordinary people do extraordinary things every day….

Activism is like a muscle: the more you use it, the stronger it'll become. It's like riding a bike: you start, you practice, you get better at it. The next thing you know, it's really not that hard.

— Loung Ung

I think [volunteering] is the most fun thing… it can be really, really amazing and rewarding and meaningful…. Sometimes I feel like it's more for me, you know? I mean, I'm not really helping them in any way near as much as they are helping me.

— Natalie Portman

Discover your fantasy of what you need the most, what you would want someone to do for you the most, and then go out and give it to someone else.

— Eve Ensler

Thoughts on Today's Feminism

First and foremost, I'm a feminist. Basically that stems from a strong belief that all people and creatures deserve equal opportunity, rights, and respect…. And I do it as a pride thing: I say, "I'm Lebanese" the same way I say, "I'm feminist" because I'm proud of being Lebanese—I think it's cool—and I think it's cool to be feminist….

I think of it as equality, choice, fairness, respect for animals and children and men and women. It's something that's based in a very loving theory for me. So I'll keep saying it as many times as I can to make up for the people who are scared to or think it's a bad vibe or whatever, because I think it's a good vibe.

—— Kathy Najimy

I get very frustrated when I hear women saying, "Oh, feminism is passé," because I think feminism means empowerment. Men can be feminists, too! Many men are feminists. We need feminism. It's not against men; it's about the empowerment of women. It's the respect of women—giving women equal rights, the same opportunities.

—— Annie Lennox

I would say a feminist is somebody who believes in personal, professional, and political equality. Period. Done. Over. It doesn't matter if you're a man or a woman or pink or yellow or whatever. Those three things. It's just equality.

—Melissa Etheridge

Feminism is my life! It's who I am. For me, it's just a logical way to be. It's the way I approach everything…. Feminism to me is like the oxygen that we breathe. It's so vitally important to life because women ultimately make life happen. So feminism is really a matter of respect for life and where life comes from and what life is and respect for women's rights and what women want and respect for the earth and really respect for the planet—just respect life itself.

—Margaret Cho

I think of feminism as the movement to liberate democracy from patriarchy. It's in the interest of men, women, the planet, the future. And it is one of the most important liberation movements in human history.

— Carol Gilligan

Today millions of young women who benefit from the struggles of their mothers and grandmothers and would not give up any of their rights don't call themselves feminists because it's not sexy. They believe that feminism is dated. They have not looked around, they are not aware that today, in the 21st century, women still do two-thirds of the world labor and own less than one percent of the assets; girls are still sold into prostitution, premature marriage, and forced labor.... In times of conflict, war, poverty, or religious fundamentalism, women and children are the first and most numerous victims. Women need all their courage today, as they needed it before.

— Isabel Allende

It doesn't matter what word we use; if it has the same content, it will be treated in the same way. There are other words—there's "womanist," there's "mujerista," there's "women's liberationist"—all mean the same thing and they get the same ridicule. I think we just need to choose what word we feel comfortable with that says women are full human beings, and whatever that word is, it will get a lot of opposition. But it will also attract a lot of support. But this is a revolution, not a public relations movement.

— Gloria Steinem

Call it what you want, but we're all fighting toward the same thing and empowering women.

— Charreah Jackson

I don't know what the word is anymore, to be perfectly honest. I don't know if [the word "feminist"] is helping us anymore or not helping us. Of course, I am a feminist and I've been a feminist. But now I'm seeing there is a new way, the third way. It's not left or right. It's not Democrat or Republican. It's a third way. And the third way to me is a shift away from these principles where dominance, occupation, invasion, and violence are the tools on which the whole planet turns and operates. The new tools would be cooperation, invitation, dialogue, and care. Care would be fundamental to the principles of the world.

— Eve Ensler

Feminism Includes Men, Too

*O*nce men realize that the gender roles are a prison for them, too, then they become really valuable allies. Because they're not just helping someone else, they're freeing themselves....

There is a full circle of human qualities we all have a right to, and they're confined to the "masculine" ones, which are seventy percent of all of them, and we're confined to the "feminine" ones, which are thirty percent. We're missing more, but they're still missing a lot. If a man fights to be his whole self—to be creative, express emotions men are not supposed to express, do jobs men are not supposed to do, take care of his own children—all of these things are part of the feminist movement.

— Gloria Steinem

*W*hat a tyranny masculinity is and patriarchy is in oppressing men's vulnerability and men's passion and men's openness and men's tenderness and men's ability to grieve and men's ability to not know and to live in the mystery and live with insecurity. I think that's what we have to open up in the whole wide world, as a general idea.

— Eve Ensler

$\mathcal{F}$eminism is for men as well as women. I cannot emphasize that enough…. I do a lot of public speaking, and I look out at the audience, and there are always men as well as women. And when I talk about this, I can just see the tension go out of the men's shoulders. It's like, "I'm included. I'm included in this." What we can do for men is help them see that [feminism] is not attacking men. On the contrary…. The opposite of patriarchy is not matriarchy—it's democracy.

— Jane Fonda

$\mathcal{S}$o many of us by now have these wonderful feminist sons and grandsons who really are allies. We should give them the respect as allies, in changing a lot of the things that are wrong and done against women in the world.

— Alice Walker

Injustice in the World Affects Us All

You know, you can't be a racist feminist, you can't be a sexist civil rights activist. You have to sort of merge the two because it's all injustice; we're all impacted by it. So the same way we're all hurt by women being put down, we're all hurt if all races aren't able to be at the table, because diversity isn't just race, it's so many other things. And you miss so much when you only surround yourself with people like you.

— Charreah Jackson

What you deny someone else, you are denying yourself. And what you deny yourself, you are denying someone else.

— Melissa Etheridge

As a woman, I'm a minority—and once other people's rights start getting taken away, it's a step toward taking mine away. So I have to, in my own self-interest, I have to try to protect the rights of others…. So it's impossible for me to think of injustice, oppression, discrimination, and non-freedom as not having to do with me—it totally has to do with me….

Things being right affects us all—caring that we live in a right world, in a just world, no matter what. You know, you can't separate yourself—no matter how much money you have, no matter how famous you are, no matter how religious you say you are, no matter how many family members you have, no matter how great a job you have—you are affected by the injustices of the world. You are, no matter what.

— Kathy Najimy

Our Most Difficult Times Can Open Our Hearts

I became aware in my own life when going through difficult times that you really have a choice in times of crisis to break down and be broken or to break open, which means to let the shock and grief of a hard time open your heart. A door opens and you have a powerful moment in time to see how you helped create the situation you are in and to deeply learn from the experience instead of blaming or feeling like a victim. Even if your difficult time comes at you out of the blue, like cancer, even those times open your heart to the magic and power of life and give you this inner commitment to live every moment. So the people I know who have been broken open through illness, even if they had a terminal illness and died from it, lived the years left to them with much more aliveness than most people who stumble and kvetch through a long life. Because life actually is this mystery and gift, and every moment of it can be full of real, radical joy and wakefulness. And for some reason in our most difficult times, we have the best chance to wake up.

— Elizabeth Lesser

We may encounter many defeats, but we must not be defeated. It may even be necessary to encounter the defeat so that we can know who we are. So that we can see, "Oh, that happened, and I rose. I did get knocked down flat in front of the whole world, and I rose. I didn't run away; I rose right where I'd been knocked down." That's how you get to know yourself. You say, "Hmm... I can get up! I have so much courage in me that I have the effrontery, the incredible gall to stand up." That's it. That's how you get to know who you are.

—Maya Angelou

What's different about me is that I've been told I was broken, and I've learned I am not. During the war, I was truly powerless. I had no voice. I had to be invisible, dumb, mute, deaf, and blind in order to survive. I know what it's like to be treated as subhuman, to live in fear. I know how devastating that was. I was a victim.

After the war, so many people heard about my story and saw me as a victim. But I didn't want their pity; I wanted their support and respect. So I stepped out of that role. I started thinking of myself as a survivor, a fighter, a warrior. There's power in that. Now I have my dignity, freedom, life back—and I'm not willing to give them up.

—Loung Ung

I always go back to my grandmother's advice to me, which was the first time I fell and hurt myself. She said to me, "Honey, at least falling on your face is a forward movement." And that came back to me many times as I failed to get the job or failed to do things perfectly or the way that I needed to do or wanted to do or whatever.... So you have to be willing to be brave enough to risk falling on your face, to risk failing.... Everything we do is about taking risks.

—Pat Mitchell

Sometimes these blows are so severe that you just think, "Well, it's not about whether I deserved it, it's just that that's what's happening." And since that's what's happening, what do you do with it? So I have, as the years have gone on, really gotten to that place where I do say to myself, "Well, wow—I bet I'm going to learn something pretty amazing right here because this is so painful or this is so strange." And that has been true!

—Alice Walker

The Path of Healing

I waited my whole life for somebody to rescue me. I waited for someone to make it better… and I created this character named Mr. Alligator who I thought would come and rescue me. I would wait for him all the time as a kid. He didn't come. But years later, my organization, V-Day, went to Africa and we found Agnes [an African woman working to stop the practice of female genital mutilation], and we were able to give her the resources to build a safe house for girls. I went to the opening of the house, and in the midst of the celebration, I found myself walking down this path. Suddenly it was the path of my childhood. In that moment, I realized that I was no longer waiting: Mr. Alligator had finally come. Here was this beautiful safe house we had opened for girls to escape female genital mutilation. In giving that, I had healed the broken part inside myself. When you give what you need the most, you heal whatever is broken. What we are waiting for has always lived inside us.

I think what I would say to anyone is: Stop waiting. Stop retaliating. Stop living your life as if you're going to be rescued, and give what you need the most. And you will heal and you will transform whatever pain is inside you.

—— Eve Ensler

*E*ach person's healing path is unique. Don't let other people hurry you. The path is different for everybody.

— Loung Ung

*L*ife is filled with suffering of all different types… and you can't escape it—no matter who you are, it doesn't matter. Suffering is an element of life. And if you do something with it, like create something, it is a very satisfying way to cope with it.

— Margaret Cho

*L*ook what you've already come through! Don't deny it. You've already come through some things, which are very painful. If you've been alive until you're thirty-five, you have gone through some pain. It cost you something. And you've come through it. So at least look at that. Have a sense to look at yourself and say, "Well, wait a minute. I'm stronger than I thought I was."

— Maya Angelou

I do believe that it is not enough to go deep in your healing, but you have to go wide as well. In the West, talk therapy often goes deep, but rarely are we ever told to go wide. When you go deep, you can get stuck in the thought that "this" is all about you. But it's not. I survived the Khmer Rouge genocide… but so did 5 million other Cambodians and 120 million others of other wars in the last century. What happened to me was not only a crime against Cambodians, but a crime against humanity. I have to keep this in mind, spread out the pain a little, or I'll drown in it. So I get involved with causes, become an activist, and cast my nets for like-minded friends and helping hands everywhere. Because going deep without a safety line to pull you out when you're in the dark, you can get lost in it. It's important to keep a foot in the world as you are going inside your heart.

— Loung Ung

[Forgiving] is one of the hardest things to do, but it's really necessary. Without forgiving, you don't really move—you can't. It's like this little prison that you're in. And it's so painful because you feel like you don't deserve to be in prison, it wasn't your fault, and how dare you have to forgive these horrible people. But actually, you do.

—Alice Walker

We have to heal the violence within ourselves as we heal the violence in the world.

—Kerry Washington

What Is Your Wish for the Children of the World?

A certain fearlessness of being who they are and expressing themselves as freely as a pear tree or an apple tree expresses itself. Just be what it is that you are, and that is *just fine*. You don't have to be what you're not in any way. Live that and live that fully, and that is where you discover ecstasy. You can't really have ecstasy as something other than yourself. And life should be ecstatic, not every minute, but you should definitely have enough ecstasy in your life from time to time to know that you are just completely wired into creation.

— Alice Walker

I wish that we could look into each other's faces, into each other's eyes, and see our own selves. I hope that children have not been so scarred by their upbringing that they only think fear when they see someone else who looks separate from them.

— Maya Angelou

Clarity and the desire for the truth and to be free from fear. To create and move this humanity to the great places that it can get to.

— Melissa Etheridge

That they are able to live in a clean, peaceful world. I do worry about my grandchildren. I have always believed that we are on an upward trajectory and that everything is for the best in this best of all possible worlds. But there are moments when you wonder where things are going. I am not a fatalist… I think people can make a difference. I do hope that their world turns out to be—I can't say better than mine, because I have had a wonderful time—but that it is not on a downward trajectory. Because I am an optimist— who worries a lot.

—Madeleine Albright

That they will live in peace with each other and that they will live in a clean and healthy environment.

—Wangari Maathai

I wish that each child felt seen… There's just such a deep need on all of our parts to really be seen. And that could be on the most basic level, like "See me, I'm hungry, I need food." Or "See me, I'm this privileged girl who looks like she has everything, but I don't feel like you authentically know who I am." Or "I'm in a family where I get unconditional love." So I think for me, that works on all these different levels I would need it to if I were to make just one wish.

—Courtney E. Martin

Caring for the Earth

The thing that I'm finding with all this is you can't stop life. You can't ask people to give everything up, and that's not what it's about. It's about finding the alternative. We created a really fantastic little system here as far as the conveniences of our lives and the way that we get to reach each other and move through the world. But now we just have to do all those things with a better mindset. We didn't create those things to ruin the world. We didn't do it consciously, like, "Oh, let's make cars so that we can burn ourselves up." That wasn't a conscious decision, but now that we know what it does do, now it's our responsibility to make the changes….

I just do as much as I can do: be aware of my energy consumption, how much power I use, how much I run the water, set my thermostat, my recycling, my car—I drive a [hybrid]. I do my carbon offsetting for my travels because I travel so much. My travel agent just basically tallies it as I go. I am trying to retrofit everything as much as possible… I try to do it consciously and as green as possible. And I am just trying to help spread the word.

— Cameron Diaz

$\mathcal{O}$ne important thing that environmentalism does is it shows us and allows us to believe the earth is a living organism. Once we comprehend that, there's no way that we can continue with the destructive behavior that we have had, because not only is it destructive to us, but it's destructive to the earth. And maybe we're not ready to care about ourselves yet, but getting the whole world to think about taking care of the earth is the beginning of taking care of each of our individual selves....

We can still be comfortable; we can still be happy. We don't have to go backward, we just need to go forward in thought. By waking up tomorrow and saying, "I live in a world that cares about the earth as a living organism, and we care about ourselves"—if I just believe that every day, and those around me believe that, then that expands out. That's where the change comes from—right there—it's just changing the way you think.

—Melissa Etheridge

We humans tend to learn from what I call "The Phoenix Process." We tend to make huge mistakes in our lives, and those are the wake-up calls. As a group, we've made a huge mistake, and it's been building forever—since the first cavemen sat around a fire, we've been contributing to global warming. We just have more humans now and stronger fires. And we will either awaken like the phoenix did from the fire into a more conscious community… or we won't. And then that will be the end of that story.

— Elizabeth Lesser

It's time to do something about [the environment]. And if we don't do it now it's going to be too late….

I think people get scared that they're not going to be able to do it perfectly, they're going to be criticized, they're going to be like, "Well, I'm not totally green." Well, you know what? At this point, we don't care. Just a shade of green is enough right now. Move a little bit closer toward this. Because the more people start moving closer and closer to it, that's something that collectively makes a difference.

— Cameron Diaz

If we all give up hope and do nothing, well then indeed there is no hope. [The planet] will be helped by all of us, every one of us, taking action of some sort.

— Jane Goodall

You can't really turn your back on the basics of how you treat each other and how you treat the earth.

— Sandra Bernhard

You cannot protect forests, you cannot protect the land, you cannot protect the environment just by having knowledge alone. You have to take action. And sometimes action means digging a hole, planting a tree, making sure that the trees are protected, making sure that our rivers remain clean, that the lakes are clean. But just having the knowledge, sometimes it doesn't help.... We need action.

— Wangari Maathai

All Life Is Interconnected

It is so important for people to understand that, especially this issue of climate change, it really does bring home the fact that we are on one planet and that some of the impact of what human beings do in one corner of the world is going to affect people in a distant corner of the world. So we may still feel very far from each other, but we are really very close to each other because of the changes we have made with travel and technology and especially information technology.

— Wangari Maathai

Everything in this life is interconnected. And things which go on in, let's say, the Congo Basin—it may seem incredibly unimportant in the Midwestern United States, but when you realize that the loss of the tropical forests in the Congo Basin is having an enormous effect on climate change, and climate change in turn is affecting weather patterns all over the world, then you start to realize that life is interconnected. Then, on the other hand, there may be some small ecosystem and there may be an endangered species; it may be an insect, and so what if it disappears? But maybe that insect is the main prey of a certain kind of bird, and if the insect goes, the bird goes; and maybe that bird was important for dispersing seeds of various plants, and so those plants will start becoming extinct. And one thing leads to another, and none of the biologists know where it's going to stop. So the answer to it really is that we know we are all interconnected and we don't yet know the effects of removing a strand from the web of life.

— Jane Goodall

We're a global society; we're a global community. Everyplace I go, everyone's the same. I go to Africa, and I just got back from Peru… and no matter what the culture is, everybody's doing the same thing. Everybody's surviving off the planet, surviving off the land somehow. That's the only way to do it. And they all want the same thing—they all have families, they all have homes, they all just want to make a living, they all want to be happy, they want to be loved.

I see it everywhere I go. There's no exception. And that's really powerful. It's really powerful to see that we really are all the same. We all need the same things, and we all get it from the same place. So in that alone, we have become a global society and what we do has an impact. What I see is all of it coming together…. It's kind of exciting to see how we all are connected now, completely connected.

— Cameron Diaz

We are so much a globe at this point that the idea that we still live as nations seems utterly absurd to me. Because it's so clear—if you look at global warming, if you look at 9/11, if you look at anything that's going on—that everything is completely interconnected and interdependent.

— Eve Ensler

The Masculine and the Feminine

The world is starting to see that the feminine balance is needed—has to be there and has to be revered—for peace. Just for life! We have to have that balance.

—Melissa Etheridge

Many women hear the word "feminine" and feel like it's a noose around their necks: "Don't hold me to a mode of behavior because I'm a woman and you think this is how a woman should act" kind of thing. That's not what I'm talking about when I use the word feminine. I like the way Jungian psychology talks about femininity and masculinity—that those forces are at play in humanity. Each human has both feminine and masculine values and drives within them. Men have the feminine, and women have the masculine—we all have those forces within us. But women certainly have more of the feminine than men do, and the feminine is more about taking care of our planet, each other, and using our limited resources for "care of" instead of "domination over."

—Elizabeth Lesser

I wish more often we could talk about the feminine and masculine located in both women and men. I think too often we end up just sort of glorifying the feminine in women in a way that, for me, feels kind of regressive.

—Courtney E. Martin

There's an imbalance, and you can really feel it in the way everything is going, I think. Sometimes I feel like it's a bit of a fallacy to try to say, "Men are violent and women are nonviolent," because I don't think that's necessarily true. But I do think there is a sort of natural balance in nature between men and women and that it's being thrown off balance by the social and economic inequities between men and women.

— Natalie Portman

You can talk about equal rights, but essentially feminism will come into wholeness when we achieve a social paradigm that allows men and women to become full human beings—rather than women muting themselves and men hardening themselves, which I think is the root of all the problems.

— Jane Fonda

I've come to realize that the ancient cultures—the original cultures, which account for 95 percent of human time on Earth—were gender-balanced and balanced with nature. If it happened before, it can happen again. The Native American cultures were probably the inspiration for the suffragist movement, for instance.... To understand that for 95 percent of human history it was different is very helpful to me in believing that it can be different in the future.

— Gloria Steinem

How Do You Create Balance in Your Life?

I'm very lucky that I live in nature. I feel really blessed that I get to be in the wildness of nature because it reminds me of the wild parts of my mind and heart. I do take time to just be alone in nature. I am grateful that I learned to meditate and do other spiritual practices starting at the age of nineteen because I can at will calm the voices in my head. That comes from having a practice, and I highly recommend it…. Those are things I do: nature and practice.

— Elizabeth Lesser

I eat really well; I love food. I try to take good care of myself. I have a wonderful group of friends who love me and support me. There are times when I overcommit or find myself in that dark place of my survivor's guilt, ashamed for the food I stole, people I hurt, lies I told to survive. I reach out to my friends. I'm not afraid to ask for help, food, a movie night, a good joke. Sometimes when I am in that dark place and feel bad about myself, I think, "I can't dishonor my friends by thinking so badly of myself. My friends are good people, and if they love me, I can't be that bad." That actually helps me. I am very blessed in that I'm surrounded by good people, good human beings.

— Loung Ung

I spend a lot of time, or as much as I can, in silence
and at home…. I think all this zipping around the
world is overrated. One of the things that I've learned
is that I need to be more rooted, and so I've been
working on that. I feel that has been so helpful to
me — to cut out movement wherever possible instead
of going here and there all the time. Talking a lot less.
Being much slower and much more grounded with my
animals, with my friends. Staying extremely simple.
Dancing more, too. Just learning to really, really love
the ordinary — that nice, well-made bowl of oatmeal in
the morning and walking with my dog… just what is
ordinary, what is simple and true.

— Alice Walker

I just do the best I can and try to make some
balance between what needs doing and what
I can uniquely do.

— Gloria Steinem

Putting Ourselves First

I try to put myself first. For me, I've had to do that. If I don't kind of put my own physical and emotional health first, then I'm not really useful to any movement, to any work of art, to any creative endeavor. I have to be aware—not selfish and self-absorbed and self-obsessed—but I have to be self-aware of what my needs are and be willing to take care of my own needs.

— Kerry Washington

I think for me one of the best ways to do self-care is to surround myself with people who are real models of it and who are also really motivated to inspire me to do it.

I also just think paying attention to my own body—I really am one of those people who gets up from the computer when my eyes are going blurry and my back's hurting. And I have tried to work on my own relationship with the idea of being productive and what that means, honoring my need to go on a walk outside in the park… and doing yoga almost every day, because I find that that's something that really feeds me. And just having a lot of joy and fun in my life.

— Courtney E. Martin

I think what you do is you learn to relax... because that's the one time when you have time to read, you have time to reflect, you have time to nourish.... So if you are careful, if you plan your work, you do find the time to nourish yourself.

— Wangari Maathai

In our society, there's a belief that a good, nurturing woman gives and gives and gives... until she drops. If she takes time off for herself, she is selfish. Too many of us buy into this belief and give and give and give until we're so exhausted we can hardly move. Then we give some more!

I've dealt with this. For a while, especially after my first book was published, I was asked to emcee events, sit on boards, and write essays and endorsements for various groups and papers. As I said yes to these requests, there was a small voice in me that kept saying, "Soon people will realize I'm exhausted and stop asking. Someone please speak up for me so I don't have to say no!" Ha!

The first thing I had to learn was to speak up for myself. I learned to say no. Then I learned to choose and pick groups whose missions match my heart and passion. I can be supportive of many groups— but I have to choose.

— Loung Ung

Connecting with Nature

It's been shown several times that contact with nature is actually important for psychological development. So children who are in a concrete jungle with little opportunity to learn about the natural world — or equally, children everywhere who are glued to their computer screens and computer games — I mean, this is becoming really frightening. What can we do about it? If you can't get the child into nature, then bring nature to the child.

— Jane Goodall

There is this global migration of people from the land and into the cities, and government and city councils need to raise awareness and try to make sure that our children are not disconnected, that we have green spaces, that we have open areas in the city, that we try to bring as much of the countryside back into the city, not only because we need it, but also because we don't want to lose that connectedness.

It is extremely important for adults and especially those who are in charge of cities to make sure that we do not lose touch with the land and with the environment.

— Wangari Maathai

I just think cities are unnatural, basically. I know there are people who live happily in them, and I have cities that I love, too. But it's a disaster that we have moved so far from nature, that people no longer notice the seasons, really.... They don't know how to plant—I mean, they would starve if they had to try to grow their own food. They have no idea. Some people think that apples grow underground and potatoes grow on trees—I mean, really! They go to the market and they buy their food there and they often have no connection to who picked the food, and that's also really heartbreaking—as a daughter of a farmworker—to feel just how much they take for granted.

—Alice Walker

I'm in awe of nature. I think it's just unbelievable, and not only is it beautiful, it's the perfect plan. It's perfection. When it's working as it's meant to, there's no flaw....

[Connecting with nature] is really important. Unfortunately, we don't get to do it very often in the nature that is truly nature. But go to the park; I love going to the park. Whenever I'm in a city, I always go to the gardens, usually the municipal gardens, and I'll just take off my shoes and put my foot right on the ground. It does connect you in a totally different way. And I like hugging trees, too. I do! It's awesome. They're alive; they're brilliant. So I'm not going to be afraid to say it: I hug trees!

—Cameron Diaz

God, Religion, and Spirituality

*M*y understanding of God is an experience. God is. That's all I know. In the Biblical tradition, it would be expressed as "Be still and know that I am God." God is the "I am" energy. Something huge is at play here—cosmic creativity, consciousness, God, whatever you want to call it. I do believe that it's a guided ride. We're on a guided tour of the universe. And God or Great Spirit or "I am" is guiding the tour.

— Elizabeth Lesser

I think that for many of us, what has happened is that we have perhaps taken some parts of the religions we were raised in, and we have incorporated them into our belief systems—with gratitude. You know, like the teachings of Jesus I really love, and I love the Gnostic Gospels and the Nag Hammadi scrolls…. But we're making a new religion. Religion is going to be more self-styled. It's going to be less and less a group thing, because we're all taking from various traditions, and we're all also open to divinity just as who we are! It's a very one-on-one kind of thing. And once you realize that you are just part of the whole thing, then you just kind of worship that and yourself and everything—all is one.

— Alice Walker

There are a lot of similar aspects in all the religions. The question is which sides of them you hold up. There is a quote by Archbishop Desmond Tutu that I often reference: "Religion is like a knife. You can either pick it up and stick it into somebody's back or use it to slice bread." I think in many ways that shows the duality of it. If you are looking for the blood-curdling parts, you can find them everywhere, but if you are trying to find the common ground, I know it is there.

—Madeleine Albright

Exactly what is God? I wouldn't even like to begin to define God; I have absolutely no idea. But what I feel, and what touches me, is a great spiritual power, which I don't even want to name. If I had to, I would say "God" because I don't know any other…. I felt it very especially out in the forest, out in nature—being part of the whole, the amazing, extraordinary universe.

—Jane Goodall

Quieting Our Minds and Becoming Still

I think that silence is the best way to get real attention, especially from the deep self. So I think the people who are in solitude in the mountains or who live in temples, the people you never hear from, you never know are there, somewhere in some deep, dark cave, meditating— I think those people are basically responsible for a lot of the sanity that we do have. In my own case, I know that what I can bring to the world comes from a world of deep silence and quiet. That is where my compass—my moral compass and my internal guide—that's where they live, in that deep quiet.

—— Alice Walker

I meditate. Sometimes I meditate by sitting, sometimes I meditate by walking… I hike a lot outdoors. For me, sometimes meditating is being on top of a mountain. But drawing inward and becoming still I think is the important thing.

—— Jane Fonda

You know what happens if you're completely still? Your mind—that little tape that's running "bup, bup, bup," all the noise—it eventually runs off the reel. And you have nothing left to think. All of a sudden, the answers are just there. I think we are way too busy, we are way too noisy… and we need some stillness in our lives.

—— Melissa Etheridge

I recommend learning how to come into the presence of stillness and vastness. Learn any form of meditation. Spend twenty minutes every day if possible in meditation, listening to the crazy monkey mind inside you and learning how to still the thoughts and discover that big, deep soulful part of yourself. If you do that, it actually becomes something that you can call up at will in a hard meeting, on a crowded subway, in a difficult conversation—you can return to that still, wise voice within.

— Elizabeth Lesser

In our modern world, things are moving so fast that I think we are all losing our balance. Furthermore, every day we are invaded by new technologies that are supposed to make our lives safer, better, more advanced—but don't—and still we revere them as false gods. We have to stop. As women, we have these natural body rhythms, instincts, intuitions, and connections to Mother Earth and to each other that this fast world discounts, devalues, and obstructs.

— Loung Ung

We Are Beautiful Just as We Are

I always thought that people told you that you're beautiful—that this was a title that was bestowed upon you, that it was other people's responsibility to give you this title. And I'm sick of waiting, people! I think that the world is pretty cruel to women in what it considers beautiful and what it celebrates as beauty. And I think that it's time to take this power into our own hands and to say, "You know what? I'm beautiful. I just am. And that's my light. I'm just a beautiful woman."

I think [beauty] is just a feeling of goodness and happiness and that you don't have to change anything. I think it's about being content and not having to fix anything or change anything or do anything—that we are perfect as we are. It's just being as you are.

—Margaret Cho

One of the most frustrating things about living in the West is meeting wonderful, fabulous, phenomenal women who don't see themselves as such. How can they not when they're so beautiful and healthy and have opportunities and are generous and kind and compassionate? How can they see themselves as anything other than phenomenal? And yet because they do, they live their lives as if they are not.

—Loung Ung

There is something going on internally with young women where although we are incredibly empowered and educated, we still haven't been able to know ourselves and love ourselves on a very deep, psycho-spiritual level. So I am really interested in how do we continue to produce these awesome, superambitious, dynamic, amazing women? But at the same time I'm just as deeply invested in how do we make sure that those women know that they don't have to be everything to all people?

There is this intrinsic nature each of us has that is really beautiful and needs to be honored. That might mean not being great at everything, and it might mean not achieving at a level that you had once expected yourself to achieve at—and throwing out that superwoman model, which I think is so damaging.

— Courtney E. Martin

We're changing ourselves to fit the world instead of changing the world to fit women.

— Gloria Steinem

Women and the Media

The media could do a much better job, that's for sure—especially the media that targets women. Women's glossy magazines, women's TV series and programs, with few exceptions, are disgusting. Human rights? They couldn't care less! Their message to women is all about consumerism, looking sexy, and pleasing men in bed. And yet they have the potential to make profound changes for the better in women's lives. In the rest of the media, there are some great advocacy journalists and programs, but they are few.

—— Isabel Allende

I think that the news can be more enlightening, richer, and more in-depth about things that matter to women…. Whether it's Social Security, bankruptcy laws, the economy, the wars—they're never looked at through a gender lens, and they all impact women differently than they do men… and we're the majority of humanity. So it's as though people who do news now act as though current events are gender-neutral, and they're not. They're not.

—— Jane Fonda

Less than 12 percent of news globally concerns women and their stories. Less than 12 percent! That's outrageous! Can you imagine in any other group thinking that was okay, especially when the group is half—more than half—of the world's population?

—— Pat Mitchell

The reason women's magazines look the way they look is much less about readers than it is about advertisers. Advertisers simply won't place ads in women's magazines unless you write about their products. Other magazines may be punished if they write negatively about some product area, but only women's magazines have to write positively or they don't get the ads in the first place. A lot that women liked very much has gone out of women's magazines—fiction and a lot of articles that aren't just about products.... Women's magazine editors have to sneak in a couple of pages here and there about something that isn't about a product. Really, they're catalogues, not magazines, and should be given away free. They're much cheaper because of advertising, but I think we would be better off if we paid for the magazines—just as we do for books—and they had what we care about in them.

— Gloria Steinem

We women are told everywhere we turn—newspapers, radio, television, magazines, books—that we are imperfect in so many ways. Be it our appearance, relationships, personalities; there seem to be so many things terribly wrong with us. But how can there be that many things wrong with us and yet here we are? We've got to sit down sometimes and look at what's right and know that what's right is not anything that the world out there can dissect. It is wholly what is in you.

— Loung Ung

What Women Bring to the World

Women often have a different way of being in the workplace and the family and the society—a more inclusive, emotionally intelligent, and compassionate way. That way has been denigrated and ignored in the places where it is most needed.

The issue for all women is to stand firm in what you know in your heart of hearts—to be exactly who you are, unapologetically and with great passion and positivity.

— Elizabeth Lesser

We bring all the qualities that men bring, and then some! We are the descendents of Ginger Rogers dancing in high heels and backwards. Fred Astaire was great, but can he dance in high heels and backwards and in a floor-length gown?

In addition to grace, beauty, intellect, leadership, we bring a connection to each other and Mother Earth. We bring our intuition, compassion, instincts. I know when my friends are having a hard time, I can sense it. Maybe because I listen. Maybe it's because every month I have to stop and observe my body and what it's going through. Whatever it is, however it works, we are in tune and we are intuitive.

— Loung Ung

There's nothing women can't do. There's absolutely nothing we can't do. We're far stronger in a lot of ways than men. And that's my message to any woman I meet: there's nothing you can't do and you know that.

Women are going to change the world. They most definitely are.

— Betty Williams

Owning Our Power

Get over the feeling that the two words don't go together—women and power. The fact is, if we don't put the two together and don't understand how power changes complexion in the hands of women, then we're not going to make it. We have to own our personal power....

Women view power differently. It's not power *over*; it's power *with*. It's about empowering others.... Generally speaking, women do it differently. It's not hierarchical; it's circular.

——Jane Fonda

What would happen if women became empowered and could lead from their core basic values? Not just put women into a structure that is up-down power, like "I have power over you," but what if women could actually influence the way power is wielded in the world from a core feminine place?

——Elizabeth Lesser

I know women are pretty powerful beings, powerful spirits. If we could only tap into and realize that, we could accomplish so much.

——Loung Ung

$\mathcal{P}$ower in our lifetimes has been defined by the dominant gender that has it. And a lot of the way they have defined power is not something we as women are comfortable with, nor would we want to carry out power in that way. So we move away from the current definitions and current manifestations of power…. We are talking about redefining it, putting a woman's perspective on power. And the good news now is we have more women leading countries and companies who are doing that, so we are actually piling up a lot of evidence that isn't just nice little feminist mythology, it's actually real. Women really do use power in a different way….

In my opinion, the most important thing as a woman leader—and I learned this early through a whole bunch of great women who were in my life (and men, I have to say)—is that if you have a position of leadership and power and you don't use it in a different way, then you're wasting it. So when people used to say to me when I was the first woman president of PBS, "Well, you know, does that mean that as a woman you're going to be a different kind of president?" And I would say, "Well, I hope so!"

—Pat Mitchell

Embracing Aging

It would help not to treat age as if it were any less of a pleasure than it was when we were six and saying, "I'm six and a half." You know, we could be saying, "I'm fifty and a half" and say it with joy. Each age is different and has different discoveries and pleasures.

— Gloria Steinem

The reason that they make us all youth-oriented and vain and try to think that if we get old we are of no use anymore is because we get wiser, and they know that. And when I say "they," I mean those who are fearful of change. We are getting older, and we are getting wiser, and we are getting freer. And when you get the wisdom and the truth, then you get the freedom and you get power, and then look out. Look out.

— Melissa Etheridge

I think we need to very intentionally have women friends, and we need to seek out women who are braver, who challenge us, who can teach us, and who together with them we can face age with more courage.

—Jane Fonda

I don't really know or care what people think about older women. That's one of the huge perks of being an older woman. I am much more alive in the moment, not looking back or ahead too much and certainly not around at what other people are saying about older women!

—Elizabeth Lesser

We are redefining every age of our lives. All of us are. I mean twenty-year-olds today, they aren't where I was at twenty, and they're in a very different world. So how can we say that we're not different, we're not a different kind of sixty- or seventy- or eighty-year-old? We are! So I'm just hoping for myself and for the women around me and that I come into contact with, I just hope that I'm still learning. As long as I'm learning every day of my life, I will never feel old. Never. And I don't feel old; I feel in my head and in my heart, I don't know, ageless! That's I think because I'm still learning and still growing as a person.

—Pat Mitchell

[Aging] is an unfortunate thing that happens. I mean, yes, you can have millions of face-lifts and all these different things that women have done to their bodies…. But personally (a) I haven't got the money for that, (b) I haven't got the time for it, and (c) there are more important things to me than how you look. I think the most important thing is to keep active and to hope that your mind stays active.

—Jane Goodall

I think the main problem people have getting older, whether they know it or not, is that you're closer to dying. We may fixate on not wanting to look a certain way, but it really is just the clock ticking, that it means, "Oh, I am not immortal!" Instead of fixating on the physical aspects of aging, it's good to contemplate the deeper source of our anxiety. That can be liberating. That being said, I don't enjoy the diminishing agility of the body! I had knee surgery last year, and I can no longer go do three yoga classes and run. You know, it's not as much fun, physically. But emotionally, it's way more fun. I am so much happier and contented and less agitated; I'm just calmer. So it's like everything in this human existence: it's a trade-off. It's like you trade the virility of the body for the agility of the spirit.

— Elizabeth Lesser

Well, I don't like getting older; I have to tell you that…. But I think that what I have loved in my life are the intergenerational activities. I teach at Georgetown. It gives me an opportunity to stay very connected with the younger generation in terms of conveying information, but also getting information from them. I have always enjoyed having people of different ages around me. I have thought that was fun. I do think that one needs to have respect for people who are older. I really do love the idea that one can respect generations.

— Madeleine Albright

The Wisdom of Other Generations

I belong to the first generation of older women empowered by education and health care. Never before have so many older women had so many resources. Our role as grandmothers is to protect young women and children, to work for peace in every way and at every level, and to improve the quality of life for everybody, not just the privileged.

— Isabel Allende

Older women have the perspective of history and therefore a sense of gratitude for the strides women have made and an understanding that they could be taken away. Older women need to keep talking about where we came from; they need to keep honoring the ancestors who were so courageous and visionary.

— Elizabeth Lesser

When I want to think about what would be the right thing to do, the fair thing to do, the wise thing to do, I can just think of my grandmother. I can always hear her say, "Now sister, you know what's right. Just do right!"

— Maya Angelou

The perception that young women don't want relationships with older women… is totally not true. Every young woman I know is craving the kind of grounded energy and wisdom that come from being friends and having mentor relationships with older women. I think sometimes they just don't know where to find them. They don't know how to initiate them, and there's just so much generational segregation in our society in general that I think it creates a situation which is kind of difficult for those relationships….

I think what I find most successful in my own life is creating relationships that cross all these generational boundaries.

— Courtney E. Martin

Part of my courage comes from being a part of a strong community of women. My mother, grandmother, great-grandmother, and other ancestors had to overcome so much to survive…. And yet, here I am— their descendant—happy, healthy, and well. I am a testament of their courage, beauty, and power.

— Loung Ung

What Is Your Life Philosophy?

$\int$ ome people live in the past, some people live in the present—which is probably the most rewarding—and some people live in the future. I live in the future, so I am always thinking, "What if?" or "This could be" or "This could change" or I am trying to understand why something happens. The great joy to me is that moment—that "aha!"—when you think, "Oh, *that's* why!" That excitement and pleasure in realizing why something is happening, how it could be different, that definitely keeps me going.

— Gloria Steinem

I just think—it's almost like a bumper sticker thing—it's like everything is going to be fine in the end, and if it's not fine, it's not the end. That's a super bumper sticker (actually I think I saw it on a refrigerator), but that's like my religion.

— Margaret Cho

I think that life is a magic carpet ride—it's amazing. Everything about it is mysterious and beautiful and touching and tragic and lovely and mystical. And we waste so much time—almost every minute—on swimming against the river. Life is about change; it never stops. It's moving, and it's moving this human body inexorably toward its demise. We, as these temporary forms of human beingness, spend most of our time swimming as hard as we can against that river. If we would turn on our backs and float on this river and look up at the sky and around at the banks— it's so beautiful! We don't have to fight it and fight each other. There's enough for everybody, and yet we're greedy and scared. So to me, the purpose of life is to enjoy it! It's to enjoy the gift and to make sure that other people have an opportunity to enjoy the gift.

— Elizabeth Lesser

It's just that I create my reality every day—my intentions, my thoughts. And that only love is real. That's it. All we can do is love each other. And once you get that, then that's your philosophy. That's it! You don't need any religiosity on top of that…. I just live that every moment, every second. It becomes clear when you start doing it every day.

—Melissa Etheridge

All of us know, not what is expedient, not what is going to make us popular, not what the policy is, or the company policy—but in truth each of us knows what is the right thing to do. And that's how I am guided.

—Maya Angelou

We each have this one life gifted to us. I feel—and
I'm not going to say this in general—but I feel that my
life is a gift that I want to try to use as wisely as I can.
I want to make use of each of these amazing days that
come my way to try to make a bit of difference—to
think things through, perhaps get new ideas, to talk
to people, to write, to do my bit. You know, you get
certain gifts, and I had a gift of speaking, lecturing,
which makes people listen. It's a gift—it's an amazing
gift. And I have the gift for writing. So I must use those
gifts, and I try to.

—Jane Goodall

I get up every morning and I'm grateful for everything
that has happened. I go through my list about being
grateful for my children and grandchildren and for
the really remarkable life that I have been able to have.
I also really do think about the fact that every day
counts. I believe that every individual counts, and so I
believe that every day counts, and I try not to waste it.

—Madeleine Albright

Are You Optimistic?

I am… I see a lot of people really wanting to do positive things in the world…. You can only be optimistic, because I don't really know how you'd wake up in the morning if you felt pessimistic. I mean, it's obviously easy to feel that way with the news—you can watch the news and it feels like it's the end of the world, very apocalyptic. So I just stay away from the news and try to find people around me who are doing positive things and look to them.

—Natalie Portman

I think you have to stay optimistic…. You do sometimes feel very discouraged, but it's also very important to remain optimistic and to see the silver lining in everything you do. Sometimes things look difficult and like there is no hope, but there is always a small glimmering of silver lining that is in everything. I always look for that and hang on to that, and before I know it, another day comes and is gone.

—Wangari Maathai

I think I'm very much an optimist. I don't think I could do my work if I didn't believe there was some kind of hope for humanity.

— Sandra Bernhard

I've circumnavigated the globe four times for the work that I do. And I have met, all over the world, women like you, women like me… and they are making monumental changes. There's where my optimism lies—that one day… the givers of life will truly become the protectors. That's what I see happening.

— Betty Williams

Yes, I'm optimistic. But I also know nothing will happen automatically. Change depends on what you and I do every day.

— Gloria Steinem

What Is Your Vision for the Future?

I love the Buddhist prayer: "May all beings everywhere be happy and free." And the second line is: "And may my practice of yoga contribute to that happiness and that freedom." For me, by saying "yoga," it's not the poses alone—because I really don't practice my yoga as much anymore—but it's saying may my practices in life, may my behaviors, contribute to that happiness and that freedom. So I think that's it: may all beings everywhere be happy and free.

—— Kerry Washington

That the abundant earth would be allowed to give to all its creatures, and it would be clean and provide peaceful abiding for all creatures.

—— Elizabeth Lesser

That everybody's just going to want to do their part… be in it for the long run, and not just think of the moment. I mean it's good to be in the moment, but depending on how many moments you want to have, you have to sort of think about what you are doing in those moments, what future that creates for you.

— Cameron Diaz

The localization of everything. So there's no more violence in our families than we want to see in the world. So that we are eating locally instead of eating meals that have traveled for a thousand miles. So that the microcosm is what we wish the macrocosm to be.

— Gloria Steinem

$\mathcal{M}$y vision of a world is one that is built on sustainable values and practices, because there won't be a world if we don't figure that one out. And there are no better people than women to save the planet, because we understand the cycles of life. So if cycles of life were applied to all our environmental and natural resource degradation, we would change where we're going.

A world where girls are valued, because they must be—they have so much to contribute—and that's the economic opportunity that the world is missing. And then a world where a woman's voice really makes a difference. Because we have a different set of values, and if we speak them and live them, then the world will reflect that. That's bound to be a more equitable and just place.

—Pat Mitchell

That people pay attention, look to their neighbors. I think we've lost so much community. I think that's one of the things I've appreciated seeing most in [the villages I've visited]: just the sense of community, where like an entire family, an entire community, they take care of each other. We've really lost that. And when you lose that on a personal level, you lose that on a global level as well. So [my wish is that we] regain that.

—Natalie Portman

I would like to see a new paradigm where holding women's bodies sacred and honoring women's lives become a priority, and that honoring the earth — because you know it is what sustains you — is a priority. And all of us really getting that *care*; the principle of caring is an extraordinarily deep value.

— Eve Ensler

I would just love for everybody to be whole — just to be whole and to enjoy it and to have joy in being whole. Wholeness comes about when you're more centered in your inner being, even when you live in this fast-moving world, and yet you can sit with your wholeness.

— Loung Ung

Illuminating Our Dreams

Our role is to dream a better world
and to work courageously to make
that dream possible.

— Isabel Allende

I think that if you just follow your heart… you can
do anything. You can have anything possible. That's
what I've experienced….

We all have the ability to do whatever we set out
to do. You just find the ways; you just create the
opportunities.

— Cameron Diaz

We have more courage, more worth,
and more strength than we realize.

— Loung Ung

We do carry an inner light, an inner compass, and the reason we don't know we carry it is because we've been distracted. We think that the light is actually being carried by a leader or somebody that we have elected or somebody that we very much admire, and that that's the only light. So we forget that we have our own light—it may be small, it may be flickering, but it's actually there. So what we need to do, I think, is to be still enough to let that light shine and illuminate our inner landscape and our dreams—especially our dreams. And then our dreams will lead us to the right way.

—Alice Walker

About the Women Included in This Book

Madeleine Albright, PhD, served as U.S. Ambassador to the United Nations and went on to become the first woman to hold the position of U.S. Secretary of State. She is a professor at Georgetown University and the author of four best-selling books.

Isabel Allende is a best-selling author, a lifelong advocate for human rights, a passionate speaker, and the founder of the Isabel Allende Foundation.

Maya Angelou, PhD, is an accomplished poet, award-winning writer, performer, dancer, actress, director, activist, and teacher. She is also a three-time Grammy Award winner for her autobiographical spoken-word recordings.

Sandra Bernhard is a comedienne, actress, singer, and author who has been entertaining and challenging audiences for more than 25 years. She is also an advocate for social causes and human rights.

Margaret Cho is a comedienne, actress, best-selling author, activist, singer, and blogger. She's won numerous awards for her efforts to promote equal rights for all people, regardless of race, sexual orientation, or gender identity.

Cameron Diaz is one of the most sought-after actresses in Hollywood. A devoted environmentalist, she traveled the world to examine environmental issues for her MTV show, *Trippin'*, and continues to raise awareness about the climate crisis.

Eve Ensler is an internationally acclaimed playwright and author best known for her award-winning play, *The Vagina Monologues*. She is the founder and artistic director of V-Day, the global movement to end violence against women and girls.

Melissa Etheridge is a two-time Grammy Award winner and a multi-platinum recording artist, as well as a human rights activist, breast cancer survivor, and 2007 Academy Award winner for best song in the documentary, *An Inconvenient Truth.*

Jane Fonda is an Academy Award-winning actress, as well as an activist and advocate for environmental issues, human rights, and the empowerment of women and girls. She is a cofounder of the Women's Media Center.

Carol Gilligan, PhD, is an internationally acclaimed psychologist, writer, teacher, and pioneer of gender studies—particularly in the psychological and moral development of girls. She is a professor at New York University.

Jane Goodall, PhD, is a world-renowned primatologist, speaker, and author. She founded the Jane Goodall Institute, as well as Roots & Shoots, a global nonprofit that empowers youths to make a positive difference for all living things.

Charreah Jackson is a blogger, writer, and editor. A proud feminist, she is a frequent speaker on achieving success and women's issues.

Annie Lennox is a Grammy Award-winning recording artist and founder of SING, a humanitarian organization that raises awareness for the AIDS/HIV pandemic in Africa.

Elizabeth Lesser is the cofounder and senior advisor of Omega Institute, the largest adult education center in the U.S. focusing on health, wellness, spirituality, social change, and creativity. She is also a host on *Oprah Radio*, a speaker, and a best-selling author.

Wangari Maathai, PhD, was the first African woman to win the Nobel Peace Prize. She founded the Greenbelt Movement, a nonprofit organization that has planted over 45 million trees across Kenya. She also cofounded the Nobel Women's Initiative.

Courtney E. Martin is a blogger, author, teacher, speaker, and editor at Feministing.com. She has appeared on the *TODAY Show*, the *O'Reilly Factor,* and MSNBC, and she has spoken on radio programs and at colleges and nonprofit organizations across the nation.

Pat Mitchell was the first woman president and CEO of PBS, the Public Broadcasting Service. She is also known for her humanitarian efforts and her work as a dedicated member of numerous nonprofit boards.

Kathy Najimy is a film, television, and Broadway actress. An activist for women's rights, AIDS, and animal rights, she has received numerous awards for her humanitarian work and has been the keynote speaker for over 50 organizations across the country.

Natalie Portman is an Oscar-nominated actress. She was named the first Ambassador of Hope for FINCA International, an organization that promotes micro-lending to empower women in poor countries by helping them start their own businesses.

Gloria Steinem is a renowned feminist activist, organizer, lecturer, and best-selling author. She cofounded *Ms. Magazine* in 1972, which has become a landmark in both women's rights and American journalism. She is also a cofounder of the Women's Media Center.

Loung Ung is a survivor of Cambodia's killing fields and an activist for the elimination of land mines. She is also a lecturer and the author of two best-selling memoirs.

Alice Walker is a best-selling author of many volumes of poetry, powerful nonfiction collections, and literary fiction, including the Pulitzer Prize-winner, *The Color Purple*. She is active in environmental and feminist causes and issues of economic justice.

Kerry Washington is an award-winning actress and activist. She serves on the board of directors for V-Day and for the Creative Coalition, a nonprofit that educates entertainers about pressing issues so they can better inform and influence their communities and the nation.

Betty Williams won the Nobel Peace Prize in 1976 for her work to bring peace to Northern Ireland. She is the founder and president of World Centers of Compassion for Children International and a cofounder of the Nobel Women's Initiative.

Acknowledgments

I extend heartfelt gratitude and appreciation to the following people: My wonderful parents, Carol and Norman Schnall, whose encouragement, love, and support allowed me to be who I am. My amazing and talented brother, Eric Schnall, with whom I've shared so much and who has always known who he is. My husband and soul mate, Tom Kay, who understands me like no other, has been the perfect copilot in my life, and has helped and supported me in countless ways. My beautiful daughters, Jazmin and Lotus—two true individuals. I have such immense love for and pride in both of you, and I feel so blessed to be your mother and to watch you blossom. My magical grandfather, Buddy Singer, who instilled in me a sense of adventure, curiosity, and a zest for life, as well as the inspiration to engage in the world and help others. The incredible women on the Feminist.com Board of Directors whose friendships and support over the years I am immensely grateful for: Karen Obel Cape, Ophira Edut, Tamera Gugelmeyer, Sheherazade Jafari, Jennifer Meyerhardt, Amy Richards, Pamela Shifman, Susan Celia Swan, and Lauren Wechsler Horn. All the extraordinary women in this book who have granted me the great honor and pleasure of interviewing them and allowing me to be the conduit for their valuable insights and wisdom. Five amazing women in particular who appear in this book, whom I have interviewed numerous times and who have acted as mentors, role models, and constant sources of inspiration for me along the way: Eve Ensler, Jane Fonda, Elizabeth Lesser, Kathy Najimy, and Gloria Steinem. All the friends and special women who have given me endless encouragement, feedback, and ideas for this book and who give me strength and enrich all other aspects of my life. The *Huffington Post*, the Women's Media Center, *Glamour*, *Entertainment Weekly's* EW.com, and *O, the Oprah Magazine,* where excerpts of some of these interviews first appeared. Blue Mountain Arts and especially my brilliant editor, Angela Joshi, for her belief and vision for this book and her tremendous help, support, and advice throughout the process.